ACCOUNTOFIT

ACCOUNTING FOCUSED ON PR**OFIT**S

ACCOUNTING **TO** BE **FIT**

BY CARL RAMQUIÑONY

© Carl Ramquiñony

Certificate:

FOLIO 03-2020-021011274700-01

INDAUTOR

First edition, 2020

Email: cpcarlosramos@cprqconsultoria.com

Web: www.cprqconsultoria.com

Editorial Design:

Enter Creativos

www.entercreativos.com / hola@entercreativos.com

This book talks about Accounting focused on Profits, the author explains in a simple way (without CPA's technical words), how to use accounting to make good analysis to increase our profit and with practical examples, teach us how to do it. And how to make a simple "Accounting System" with Excel.

The word ACCOUNTOFIT is a combination of ACCOUNTING and PROFIT, but also ACCOUNTING and FIT, to be healthier, to have healthy finances. This book tells us how we can use Accounting to correctly analyze information in a way that helps generate more profits.

SALTILLO, COAHUILA

DEDICATION

To my family and to all the entrepreneurs that need to understand the numbers of their business in order to make good decisions, because my goal is to help business and entrepreneurs to increase their profits.

ACKNOWLEDGMENTS

To my parents, Dr. Carlos Ramos and Dr. Lupita Quiñones, who are the two persons that I most admire. Thank you for educated me with your example and values, that made it easier for me to relate with extraordinary people.

To my wife Diana for supporting me, take care of me, understand me and for being (together with my children Carlos, Mariana and Patricio) what I love the most and the reason why I always seek to improve myself.

To my Grandma María, because she is the one who prays the most for me. Although I had to teach her how to pray, because she only asked "work" for me ... and there I was working late until Saturdays and Sundays. I already told her to ask for Health, Love and Money, I'll take care of work.

To my sisters, aunts, uncles, cousins and all my relatives that always support me.

To my friends and compadres, they are few, but they are enough because they are excellent people.

CONTENTS

I.- INTRODUCTION

℧his book was made for entrepreneurs of micro, small and medium size businesses. The goal is that Accounting can help them analyze their business and increase their profits. It is not for CPAs, since the language used in this book is the common language, not the one used by Accountants normally when they analyze business.

This is a small book, easy to understand and with practical examples that we can use immediately in our business to make good analyzes and increase our profits.

I think it is easier to understand a short book since we are used to receive information quickly and sometimes we get desperate when it is not like that and we leave the book aside. It was a challenge to summarize what I have learned in 20 years and put it in a common language, since the Accountants use many technical words and that was the way I was taught through many classes, courses, workshops, books and in work.

Let me tell you briefly about myself, I'm a CPA, Master in Finance, I worked for 20 years as an Accountant, Controller, CFO and Business Consultant mainly for large companies in Mexico and in the United States. I am currently a Business Consultant and what I tell you in this book is what has been most useful for my clients, which is to use the information to analyze it correctly to make decisions that increase their profits.

Accountofit means Accounting focused on profits, since accounting can be used for different reasons such as to calculate / pay taxes, to apply for a loan or other reasons, but it can also be used to increase profits and this is the approach we will give to Accounting in this book.

The word Accountofit also means Accounting to be fit, to be healthy, to be financially healthy, since with the correct information and constantly measuring adequate indicators of the business you can have healthy finances.

II.- DIFFERENT KINDS OF ACCOUNTING.

$\mathfrak{A}$ccounting is a way, a technique, of recording business information in an orderly manner that allows us to make reports (Financial Statements) for different reasons or purposes and that is why there are different kinds of accounting.

I will briefly talk about the different reasons why accounting is made to see the differences between them:

1.- The main reason why accounting is made, is to calculate and pay the TAXES, since it is something required by the Government and mandatory for all businesses, so we must do it if we don't want to have problems with the IRS. The Tax Accountant helps us to make the accounting in order to comply with tax obligations and to pay the least amount of taxes possible.

The Government tells us to include all the invoices that our customers pay us, as well as those that we pay to our suppliers with the only objective of paying taxes based on our profit. However, the government does not care in which products we have profits and in which products we have loses or if the customers owe us or not invoices. That is why the reports obtained from this information are global and we cannot use them to make analyzes that help us make decisions to increase profits.

Another thing that doesn't help us in the analyzes is that sometimes we include some expenses that are not from the business in order to pay less taxes, as wife's gasoline, house cleaning supplies or other personal bills that are not from the business. So we include expenses that are not from the business, obviously the reports and analyzes that we make with this information cannot be considered for business decision making.

As a summary of this point, tax accounting is very important because it is mandatory by the Government, but it does not help us to have adequate information to make good decisions and increase our profits.

2.- Another reason to make accounting is to **request a loan** and this is similar to the one for taxes purposes because it is done globally, since the only goal is to get the authorization of the loan by the Bank or the lender and since we don't have detailed information by product/project/process, we cannot use these reports for decision making.

3.- There may be several more reasons, but the reason to make accounting that we are looking for and the one related to the word "Accountofit" is **to increase profits** and for this purpose we need to record the business data in a detailed way (by product, project or process) to make adequate analyzes that show us the right "picture" of the business so we can make the right decisions for the business.

These decisions will help us to correct situations in which there are opportunities, as well as continue doing and improve what is being done correctly.

The picture that I'm talking about is that the numbers can show us the reality of the company in a clear and detailed way so we can see practically an image of our business and based on that, see what went well in the picture and what went wrong, in order to make the corrections needed.

That picture should tell us the size of the company, what sales and costs we have, what profits or losses are generated each month, as well as what we have, what is owed and how they were generated in the business.

However, this reason to make accounting, since it is not mandatory by the Government, we do not pay attention to it most of the time. Because we are busy in operational, administrative, sales or tax matters and we do not realize the importance of making good analysis to improve our finances.

SUMMARY
KINDS OF ACCOUNTING:
1.- For Taxes.
2.- For Loans.
3.- To Increase Profits

II.- MAIN FACTORS TO TAKE AND ANALYZE THE PICTURE (ACCOUNTING).

𝕿o be able to take and analyze the business picture, three things are mainly required:

1.- Record the information correctly

Before taking the picture, we must prepare the environment for it. It would be the part where the lights and cameras are placed in the right position to make a good shot.

In this part we must record with the detail that our business requires (by product, project or process) and ensure that we do not miss information. What is recommended is to go through the entire operational and administrative process to check that we do not skip recording any activity and any expenses.

It is important that we define what will be the detail that we want to register, so we can make a list of accounts (or chart of accounts as the CPAs call it) that we are going to use. If you don't know anything about accounting, don't worry, since we are going to see a practical and simple example to understand it.

Each business is different and we must make the records based on the detail required for each business. Some will require detail by product, others by project, and others by customer. For example, there are businesses that all the sales are in cash, so accounts receivable from customers are not relevant, but there are other business who sell on credit and accounts receivable must be constantly measured, since based on this, they will have the cash flow available to operate the business.

It is important that we record everything properly and that we don't miss any information, since it is common to make certain types of errors when we make the accounting. For example, we must identify which operations that aren't related with money we need to include, such as the depreciation of our own machinery or building. Since it is important that we consider this type of expenses, because these assets deteriorate and lose value when we use them.

It is also common that we don't record a salary for the owner, however it is necessary that we consider it (even if it is not paid).

Sometimes we do not record lease expenses because the office/building belongs to a relative (father or mother) who doesn't ask for any payment, but in order to evaluate ourselves as a business, it is necessary to consider it. For example, if my profit is $1,000 dollars per month and I am using my parents building for free, but if other offices/buildings like the one that I have pay leases of $1,500 dollars, It would be better for me to lease that building to someone else and get the $1,500 dollars per month. I would earn more and I would not be investing (or wasting) my time and effort.

We must pay attention to these kinds of situations, especially when they involve time from us. There is a comment that made me laugh at the time, but it did happen to me "there are people who are more productive sleeping than going to work." And it happened to me at the beginning when I was prospecting some customers. I did it with great enthusiasm, but without good technique and sometimes I made visits to clients where at the end of the interview I realized that they could not hire my services (when I could knew that with some questions before the interview). I would have been more productive, at least I wouldn't have spent the gas in my car, or my time, if I had stay in my house sleeping.

It takes some practice to be able to take the picture correctly and although systems are generally used for it, we can use Excel to do it. We will make a complete example of how you can do it in your business in following pages.

We must remember that in any system, even the most sophisticated one, if we put garbage into the system, we will get garbage from it. This means that if we don't record the information correctly, the reports we obtain from the system will not be useful to make decisions.

SUMMARY
III.- MAIN FACTORS TO TAKE AND ANALYZE THE PICTURE (ACCOUNTING).
1.- Record the information correctly.
* Make the list of accounts for our business.
* Recording correctly and don't miss any information.

2.- Define the Reports that we will use to analyze the business (take the picture).

It is important to have the appropriate Reports or Financial Statements (as the CPAs call it) and we must include the detail that is required for each business. We defined this detail from the previous point in our list of accounts, but we must ensure that our reports show us that detail. For example, we may be interested in the amount of inventory we have of each product (or those of greater volume) and we must be able to see this in the reports or Financial Statements.

The main reports are the Balance Sheet, the Income Statement and the Cash Flow. If you don't know about this, don't worry, we will explain those Reports in a very simple way and in following pages we will make a practical example to understand it better.

BALANCE SHEET

The Balance Sheet is the report that has the most complete information, it is the one that gives us the total picture of the business.

The Balance Sheet is the report that shows the economic and financial situation of a business at a certain date. This report is accumulative, this means that it shows us the accumulated amounts up to a certain date.

This Report has three main areas, the Assets that is what the company has. The Liability that is what the company owes and the Equity that are the contributions of the partners plus the accumulated profits of the company.

A simple Balance Sheet is like the following figure where the Assets are placed on the left side and the Liabilities are placed on the right side together with the Equity:

Balance Sheet

ASSETS	LIABILITIES
	Suppliers
Banks	Lomg Term Debt
Accounts Receivable	**TOTAL LIABILITIES**
Inventories	EQUITY
Fixed Assets	Owner's investment
	Retained earnings
	TOTAL EQUITY
TOTAL ASSETS	**TOTAL LIABILITIES + EQUITY**

* Figure 1

Equity = Assets – Liabilities

Or in other words:

The Business is = What it has – What it owes.

In real life this Report have more accounts and details per customer or product based on each business needs and how they want to see the picture more clearly to make good decisions. But right now we only need to understand what this report is for.

CASH FLOW

One of the main accounts in the previous Report (Balance Sheet) and in all business is "Bank" (or Cash), that is located in the assets section on the left side of the Balance Sheet. Because of the importance of this account to analyze and control it, a separate report with the detail is needed and it's called Cash Flow.

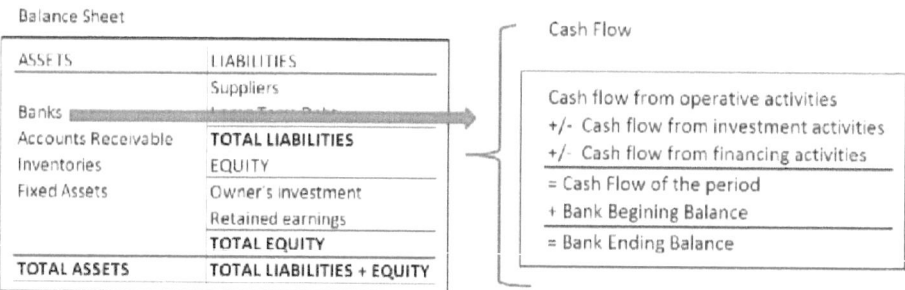

* Figure 2

This report shows the liquidity of the business, this means, the money that really comes in and out of the business. And this is a report that is made for a period of time, which is usually for a month. Unlike the previous report (Balance Sheet) that shows the accumulated activity at a certain date, this report shows the activity of one month.

What this report does is to separate the inflows and outflows of money segregating them if they were related to business operation activities or if they were related to investment or financing activities. The sum of the flows of these three activities is called the cash flow of the period.

The Initial Cash Balance is added to the cash flow of the period and we get the Final Cash Balance (what we have in Banks at the end of the month), which is the same amount as the previous report (General Balance) has in "Banks"

Cash Flow

Cash flow from operative activities
+/- Cash flow from investment activities
+/- Cash flow from financing activities
= Cash Flow of the period
+ Bank Begining Balance
= Bank Ending Balance

* Figure 3

In real life, each activity (operation, investment and financing) have more detail based on the needs of each business, but right now we only need to understand what this report is for.

INCOME STATEMENT

Another part of the Balance Sheet is of great importance is the "Retained earnings" that is in the Capital section (on the right side) and due to its importance a separate report is made to analyze it, which is the Income Statement.

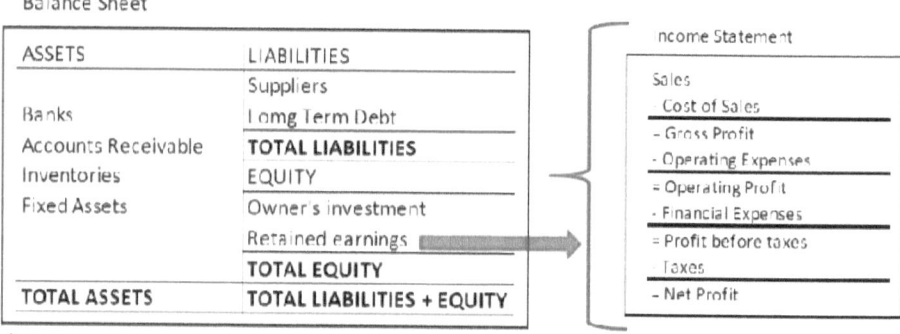

* Figure 4

The Income Statement, shows us the profit or loss that the company had in a period of time, which is normally used one month, but can be analyzed by two months, semester, year, etc.

A simple way to show it is as follows:

Income Statement

```
Sales
- Cost of Sales
---------------------------
= Gross Profit
- Operating Expenses
---------------------------
= Operating Profit
- Financial Expenses
---------------------------
= Profit before taxes
- Taxes
---------------------------
= Net Profit
```

* Figure 5

But normally in companies each of these accounts have sub-accounts so they can make a more detailed analysis based on the needs of the business.

This report is the most used to make the analyzes since it shows us the real result of the business, it gives us more clarity of the profitability of the business by removing collection noise or other situations of money movements that does not allow us to see clearly if we win or if we lose. For example in one month we could have few sales and many expenses (obviously this generates a loss), but a customer made a large payment and therefore we can think that in that month the business did it well because we brought cash, however we had loss and we must take actions to correct this.

Obviously it is very important that we collect the money from our customers, but we must see each report separately, because each one has a different purpose. The best thing that we can do is to analyze the three reports (Balance Sheet, Income Statement and Cash Flow) at the same time, in one side see the Cash Flow where we make sure that we have the necessary resources for the operation, on other side see the Income Statement where we look the real profit or loss of the month and on the other side we see the complete picture of what we are (what we have less what we owe) with the Balance Sheet, with the objective that we have the clear picture of our business and we can make decisions based on it.

More detail (by customer, product or project) should be needed in accounts where the business requires more attention. Although in real life most of the businesses focus only on the Cash Flow, since it is the one requested by the IRS, but as we mentioned earlier, in the information we register for taxes we include some non-business expenses (such as wife's gasoline) and we do not include expenses that are of the business (such as depreciation, rent because the building is from our parents, etc.) and obviously these reports cannot help us to analyze the business and make decisions.

SUMMARY

III.- MAIN FACTORS TO TAKE AND ANALYZE THE PHOTO (ACCOUNTING).
2.- Define the reports that we will use to analyze the business (take the picture).
There are three main Reports or Financial Statements:
* Balance sheet.
* Cash Flow.
* Income Statement.
To make a correct analysis you must see the three reports.

3.- Analyze the reports monthly (analyze the picture).

After taking a good picture, it's necessary to analyze it and we need to have some practice to do it, this is why we'll do an exercise in following pages. Being able to analyze business numbers is not something simple, but every time we do it, becomes easier and more productive.

It's like the movie "The Matrix" in which on a screen you can see green numbers that run from top to bottom and we don't know what they say, however "Tank" the person who constantly look at the monitor, sees them perfectly and tells "Neo" where a building is located, the stairs, a telephone booth, etc.

The same happens when we analyze the picture (the business reports), we require experience to know what numbers / information are the ones that we should pay attention, to be able to read it and make appropriate decisions to increase the profits of the business.

Not all businesses are equal, so you must analyze which are the metrics that should pay attention in each business. It is important to follow up and have discipline, to have monthly results meetings where action plans are defined and follow up on them.

There are several metrics that we can analyze that CPAs call financial indicators, which allow us to measure how our business is doing. There are many metrics and it varies on the situation of each business to know which ones to use, but the ones that are used most frequently are the following:

1.- Return on investment. What is measured with this indicator is the amount we have of profit compared to the investment that was made. This helps us to compare it against the performance that the bank or other investment would give us for that same amount of money. In other words, how much we earn in our business compared to having invested the money in the Bank or another investment (which could be in someone else's business). The profit (interest) that the bank gives us is low, normally the maximum that we can get from the bank is 6% per year, although there are other investments or third-party businesses that can give us a 30% per year. We can use these percentages as a basis to know if what our business give us is good or not.

If we have an annual return on investment less than the 6% that the bank can give us, it is better for us to put the money in the bank than operate the business. Sometimes the building is ours and it would be better for us to rent it than to continue operating.

We must be clear that we are not talking about the % of annual profit vs sales, because that percentage could be greater than 6% per year. We are talking about the % of profit vs the investment.

If at any time we choose to invest in the business of a third party, we must consider that at higher profits, we have higher risks. So the project must be evaluated in detail before making a decision. There are good projects in the market, we get some projects with good returns and sometimes they require investment and as those there should be many projects, you just need to evaluate them correctly.

Return on investment = Profit / Investment

2.- Percentage of Profit on sales, this metric helps us to know how is our profit compared with the sale, this is one of the main indicators, since it tells us how much we are earning or losing in our business. This indicator should be measured monthly and set objectives and action plans based on their results. Many businesses want this indicator to be above 15% monthly, although there are more aggressive businesses that look for a 25% monthly or more.

% Profit on sales = Profit / Sales

3.-Percentage of Gross Profit, this indicator tells us how our cost is compared with the sale. The cost includes mainly the materials and direct labor that we need to produce.

% Gross Profit = Gross Profit / Sales

To set a goal in this metric it is necessary to see the kind of business and industry that we have, since it is very variable from business to business and can have ranges that goes from 90% to 30% of gross profit. To know if this percentage is good or not, we must see the other expenses that we have and that the Total Profit can be in the range that we mentioned in the previous point.

4.- Current Ratio is one of the most used indicators for solvency, its purpose is to verify the possibilities of a company to face financial commitments in the short term.

Current Ratio = Current Assets / Current Liabilities.

5.- Accounts receivable turnover is a metric that tell us the time it takes for accounts receivable to become cash, or in other words, it is the time it takes for the business to collect from the customers.

AR Turnover = (Accounts receivable x 360 days) / Sales

The accounts receivable turnover allows us to identify how long it takes us to recover sales on credit, this data is important to know how many days we are financing our clients, since that has a financial cost.

6.- Break Even Point, is an indicator that tells us how many units we must sell in order not to lose or win, that means, the necessary sales in units to cover the costs and all the expenses of the business.

Break Even Point = Fixed Expenses / (Unit Price - Unit Cost)

This metric allows us to see what is the minimum quantity of sales we should have and compare it against current sales.

We must consider that all the metrics are changing month by month, including the Break Even Point, since it can increase or decrease if the fixed expenses, the unit price or the unit cost are modified. So we must measure them constantly, at least once a month.

There are many more metrics or indicators and we should use the ones that are better to analyze our business.

Besides those metrics, trends or comparisons of the information between the different months or years can be used to analyze the business, for example we can see how this month sales are compared with the previous month or a specific month, and this same type of comparisons can be made with the main expenses.

If we analyze the business frequently we'll get more used to the numbers, we will have greater clarity of the business and that will help us make successful decisions quickly.

SUMMARY

III.- FACTORS TO TAKE AND ANALYZE THE PHOTO (ACCOUNTING)
3.- Analyze the reports monthly (analyze the photo).
There are several metrics that can be analyzed, among the most common are:
1.- Return on Investment.
2.- Percentage of Profit on Sales.
3.- Percentage of Gross Profit.
4.- Current Ratio.
5.- Accounts Receivable Turnover.
6.- Break Even Point.

Besides metrics, trends or comparisons of information between different months or years can be analyzed.

IV.- KEY FACTORS TO ENSURE BUSINESS SUCCESS

𝕴n addition to what we have previously said on Rerecording properly, Define the Correct Reports and

Analyzing those reports so that we can make good decisions, there are other factors that are necessary for the success of the business:

1.- Monthly Results Meeting. We must have a meeting at least once a month with the Accountant, the Administrator and the Owner to see the Metrics and Results of the Business where we can make action plans and follow up to ensure the proper operation of the business.

If we do not define dates for those meetings to review the business numbers, all the work of having good records and reports will be a waste of time, since we will not be analyzing the business because we are busy in production issues, suppliers, payrolls, etc and nobody will review the numbers and obviously nobody will be able to make proper decisions in the business.

There are companies that hire Business Consulting services only to ensure to have those meetings and that they are effective.

2.- Time measurement. Another factor that we commonly see in business is that many times we do not measure the time of the main activities and therefore we don't allocate correctly that time to the cost of our products / projects. Many times, we do not measure the time that the owner uses in the activities and his/her time is, or should be, the most expensive one. Sometimes we don't measure the time of the administrator's, staff or operational activities.

To measure the time it is not necessary to have sophisticated software or a time measurement app. We don't need to count the exact minutes for each activity, because the goal is not to make it complicated, since many times in one hour we do several activities or we receive / make several calls with customers and suppliers. What we must do is a simple format in which we will record the main activities of the day by project, product or client and the time that we use for various activities will be recorded as general activities (of all products / projects / customers).

Later we will see how these general expenses are assigned to the costs of the products or projects.

3.- Control inventories and material variances. It is important that we keep track of inventories, in which we constantly (at least once a month) make physical inventories and that the variations or adjustments can be analyzed, measured and included in the costs or expenses of the business. Sometimes we do not make inventories or we do not record the adjustments and this can generate considerable expenses that we miss to analyze and therefore make decisions about it, which generates losses that we don't see and obviously we don't try to correct.

Many businesses don't make inventories constantly because they don't want to stop operation for one day every month, however it is not necessary to stop the operation to make inventories, it can be done through Cyclic Inventories, in which materials and products are segregated in groups "A, B, C, etc" based on their volume, turnover or value. Inventories of the A products are programmed on a certain day, the B products on another and so on with the other products, so that partial inventories are made on several days of the month without having to stop production any day.

In businesses that manufacture products there is a very special situation because most of these businesses use a standard costing system, in which projected or standard costs are defined for each product.

Standard costing is a good way to cost the products for this kind of business, since we define what is normally spent to produce in terms of materials, labor, etc. and this helps us to make business numbers.

However, if we don't analyze material variances, such as inventory adjustments, price increases, volume increases, etc. We will not have the costs properly and this can have serious consequences for our business. What we must do to avoid this kind of risk is that we analyze these accounts in the monthly results meeting and if we have variations, we can make the necessary correction plan.

4.- Follow up. Another very important thing is that we follow up on the action plans that we agreed in the monthly meetings. It is common that we get busy in other activities and that we don't do what we said in the monthly meeting. That is why we must follow up to do it, since if in the meeting was defined as an important activity, it is because it must be done for the business improvement.

There are activities that due to their importance should be monitored weekly or even daily, depending on the urgency.

5.- Discipline. This is something indispensable in every business and with that I mean the constancy to do things. If we said that we will have a monthly meeting, we must do it every month, if we stop doing it one time, we will stop doing it later and if we are not constant, we will not be able to make correct analyzes, we will not be able to make appropriate decisions and this is a very big risk for our business.

The same happens to measure time, to make inventories, for follow up meetings, etc. We must have discipline to do it on the dates we define for it and be constant.

6.- Business structure, last but not least, is that we can have a good business structure and this has several parts:

A.- Mission. All businesses, even micro businesses must have a mission, since it is what defines them, it is their guide, it is what the business is looking for. And what the business is looking for should not be money (that will come later), the business should seek to do something for society, at least to their potential Market even if it's a small group of people.

For example, Google's Mission is "to organize the information of the world and make it universally accessible and useful". Obviously the company generates a lot of profits, but it is important that all managers and employees of all levels know and feel committed to the company's Mission.

Besides the Mission, companies have a Vision, which is where they see themselves in the future. It is important that all staff know what is the target of the company, so everyone collaborates on it.

And in order to do this, the values of the company must be defined. As an example, if the vision is to reach 100,000 products sold per year, it shouldn't be deceiving customers with bad products, which is something that some companies do, but they don't remain for a long time doing business.

Some companies use values such as honesty, excellence, humility, etc. as the basis for achieving their vision. In my point of view honesty and humility are indispensable in every business, they are not something that is optional, if the person does not have these values, it is better that we let him/her go. I think that honesty is very clear to everyone because if there is no trust, we can't make a good team with that person. But with the word humility, sometimes we don't understand why it is so important.

By saying humility I mean that we see others as equals. And I know that nobody is equal, we are all different, but we are all people and we should not feel superior to anyone because we have a College degree, or if we have a better economical position or because we have a different race, stature or color. When someone feels superior to other people, causes that the teams don't work together and we can't let this happen in a business.

It is very important that businesses have a mission, vision and values that guide each of their members in their actions, although many companies don't have them in writing and some of those who have them, don't communicate them properly to all their people or they don't follow it.

B. Team, the human resource is the most important asset of the business and it is necessary to choose (hire) in an appropriate way. We have to invest time in hiring, we must make a list of questions for each position and at least interview 3 persons qualified for the position (for key positions must be at least 5 persons). We should not hire quickly for urgency. There are businesses that get desperate and they grab the first person that is walking through the street, but that is expensive. If you have an urgency because one of your key persons left the business, it is better if you temporarily hire an outsourcing firm or subcontract that position to do these activities, while bringing the right person.

The people we hire must share our values and be aligned with the mission and objectives of the business.

The opposite happens when we need to let go somebody from our team. If we realize that he/she is not the right person, we should immediately let him/her go from the team, because if we don't do it, that will cause problems to the team and to the business.

That's why there is a saying "hire slow and fire fast". The slow hiring means that it is a slow process because of the time we need to invest in preparing the right questions for the interview, that we are going to interview several people for the position, etc.

You should also know that having the right person has a cost and this should be considered in the planning of your business, because many times we want to hire at the lowest cost (even below Market) with the idea of "developing the person", but that could be expensive if the person don't make all the activities required by the business.

It's important that we can develop people from the lower levels of the organization, this means that we give them the opportunity to fill other positions, as long as we have someone with the technical capabilities to train that person. Because if we give someone the opportunity of a higher position, but we don't train him for it, that will generate problems for us.

The team must have Leaders, who are responsible for their areas (production, administration, etc.) and they must be empowered by the owner. By empowered I mean that they are fully responsible and can make decisions in their areas. The Owner should not give orders, but suggestions to their Leaders, because that is why he hired people for those positions.

C. Business Owner. It is common for the Owner to get involved in production, administration and finance activities, but this is why he don't have time to do the business strategic activities, such as looking for new customers, eliminating toxic customers (which take a long time to pay, requiring discounts, etc), find new suppliers, negotiate with existing suppliers, find alliances with other businesses, find new business units, etc.

It is not efficient that the Owner makes production, administration or finance activities, since these activities can be done by someone else. However, no one else can do the strategic activities, so if the Owner doesn't do them, nobody will do them and the business will never grow the level that could do it.

In some companies (and this should be the goal), business owners don't even work on a day-to-day basis and have a **general leader** or manager who executes the operation and strategic activities. Although they don't have to work much anymore, business owners are smart about how they structure their business.

Being a Business Owner it is not about working hard, but working smart.

In my opinion, the activities that the Owner must do (while he empower the general leader to do it) are:

* Perform strategic business activities.

* Perform the hiring of leaders.

* Ensure investment and initial flow.

* Structure the business as well as the legal, fiscal and financial areas.

* Make initial relationships with customers and suppliers.

We can make a network with other people where we can make a kind of society that strengthens us, in our business we have a very good relationship with Public Notaries, Tax Accountants, Lawyers, Actuaries, Insurance Agencies, Advertising Agencies, etc. , where we support each other to provide a better service to our customers.

D. Legal. It is an indispensable activity for the business, there are several legal activities, since the Company charter and all legal situations with employees, customers and suppliers. Each person must do what they are entitled to and what they are prepared to do. It is common for the Owner to negotiate settlements and as he does not have the preparation for this, he pays more than he should or does things that harm the business in lawsuits.

You can hire internal personnel to make these activities, but what most business does is to hire a Law Firm or an external Lawyer.

E. Taxes. This activity is mandatory from the Government for the business and not doing it implies a risk to operate, which is why companies gives the importance it deserves. A firm is commonly hired to do the taxes, although personnel can also be hired directly to make these activities.

F. Financial. This activity is necessary to analyze the business and make decisions to increase profits. Because this activity is not mandatory from the Government, sometimes the companies don't do it, but it is very important for the success of the business and to do these activities you can hire internal personnel, an outsourcing firm or an external consultant.

These three activities (Legal, Taxes and Financial) can be done internally, although for small and micro companies is better to hire an outsourcing Firm or an external to do it in order to lower the costs of payroll of experienced personnel plus their benefits and Social Security.

SUMMARY
IV.- KEY FACTORS TO ENSURE BUSINESS SUCCESS.
1.- Monthly Results Meeting.
2.- Measure the time.
3.- Control inventories and material variances.
4.- Follow up.
5.- Discipline.
6.- Business structure, which has the following factors or activities:
A.- Mission.
B. Team.
C. Business Owner.

D. Legal.
E. Taxes.
F. Financial.

V.- PRACTICAL EXAMPLE

So far we have seen the theoretical part, now let's see an example of what that we mentioned in previous pages with an example of a business. Let's imagine that we have a small restaurant and that we only make Sandwiches and Hamburgers and to make it simple both products only have two ingredients, which are Bread and Ham for Sandwiches. Bread and Meat for Hamburgers.

Let's do steps 1, 2 and 3 that we mentioned before to take the picture:

1.- Record the information correctly.

2.- Define the reports that we will use to analyze the business (take the picture).

3.- Analyze the reports monthly (analyze the picture).

In point 1 we said that it is necessary to make a list of the accounts with the detail that we need for the business. So I will make a simple list of accounts that is used for the Taxes approach. Normally a number is assigned to each account in which the Assets generally begin with number 1, Liabilities with 2, Equity with 3, Income with 4, Costs with 5, Expenses with 6 and Financial Expenses with the number 7:

Number	Kind of Account	Account
100.000	Assets	Assets
101.010	Assets	Cash
102.010	Assets	Banks
105.010	Assets	Accounts Receivable from Customers
115.020	Assets	Inventory - Materials
115.030	Assets	Inventory - Production in progress
115.040	Assets	Inventory - Finished goods
118.010	Assets	Taxes
152.010	Assets	Fixed Assets (Building, Machinery and Equipment)
171.010	Assets	Accumulated Depreciation
200.000	Liabilities	Liabilities
201.010	Liabilities	Suppliers
207.010	Liabilities	Taxes to pay
252.010	Liabilities	Loan from Bank
300.000	Equity	Equity
301.010	Equity	Owner's investment
304.010	Equity	Profit from previous years
305.010	Equity	Profit of the actual year
400.000	Income	Income
401.010	Income	Income
500.000	Costs	Costs
501.030	Costs	Materials
501.060	Costs	Direct Labor
600.000	Expenses	Expenses
601.010	Expenses	Salaries
601.340	Expenses	Professional Fees
601.450	Expenses	Leases
601.480	Expenses	Gasoline
601.490	Expenses	Travel Expenses
601.500	Expenses	Telephone and Internet
601.510	Expenses	Water
601.520	Expenses	Electricity
601.530	Expenses	Security guards
601.540	Expenses	Cleaning supplies
601.550	Expenses	Stationery
601.560	Expenses	Maintenance
601.570	Expenses	Insurance
601.580	Expenses	Other taxes
601.610	Expenses	Marketing
601.620	Expenses	Training
601.720	Expenses	Freight
613.010	Expenses	Depreciation
700.000	Financial Expenses	Financial Expenses
701.040	Financial Expenses	Interests
701.100	Financial Expenses	Bank fees

* Figure 6

In this example we will assume that we want to analyze it by product, this means, to separate it by Sandwich and Hamburger and that we also need to measure the quantities of each material separately. Then we will add more accounts that in the Taxes approach we don't have. These accounts are marked to identify them:

Number	Kind of Account	Account
100.000	Assets	Assets
101.010	Assets	Cash
102.010	Assets	Banks
105.010	Assets	Accounts Receivable from Customers
115.020	Assets	Inventory - Materials
115.021	Assets	Inventory - Bread for Sandwich
115.022	Assets	Inventory - Ham
115.024	Assets	Inventory - Bread for Hamburguer
115.025	Assets	Inventory - Meat
115.030	Assets	Inventory - Production in progress
115.040	Assets	Inventory - Finished goods
118.010	Assets	Taxes
152.010	Assets	Fixed Assets (Building, Machinery and Equipment)
171.010	Assets	Accumulated Depreciation
200.000	Liabilities	Liabilities
201.010	Liabilities	Suppliers
207.010	Liabilities	Taxes to pay
252.010	Liabilities	Loan from Bank
300.000	Equity	Equity
301.010	Equity	Owner's investment
304.010	Equity	Profit from previous years
305.010	Equity	Profit of the actual year
400.000	Ingresos	Income
401.010	Income	Income
401.011	Income	Income Sandwich
401.012	Income	Income Hamburguer
500.000	Cost	Cost
501.030	Cost	Materials
501.031	Cost	Materials Sandwich
501.032	Cost	Material Hamburguer
501.060	Cost	Direct Labor
501.061	Cost	Direct Labor Sandwich
501.062	Cost	Direc Labor Hamburguer
600.000	Expenses	Expenses
601.010	Expenses	Salaries
601.011	Expenses	Salaries Sandwich
601.012	Expenses	Salaries Hamburguer
601.340	Expenses	Professional Fees
601.341	Expenses	Professional Fees Sandwich
601.342	Expenses	Professional Fees Hamburguer
601.450	Expenses	Leases
601.451	Expenses	Leases Sandwich
601.452	Expenses	Leases Hamburguer

Number	Kind of Account	Account
601.480	Expenses	Gasoline
601.481	Expenses	Gasoline Sandwich
601.482	Expenses	Gasoline Hamburguer
601.490	Expenses	Travel Expenses
601.491	Expenses	Travel Expenses Sandwich
601.492	Expenses	Travel Expenses Hamburguer
601.500	Expenses	Telephone and Internet
601.501	Expenses	Telephone and Internet Sandwich
601.502	Expenses	Telephone and Internet Hamburguer
601.510	Expenses	Water
601.511	Expenses	Water Sandwich
601.512	Expenses	Water Hamburguer
601.520	Expenses	Electricity
601.521	Expenses	Electricity Sandwich
601.522	Expenses	Electricity Hamburguer
601.530	Expenses	Security guards
601.531	Expenses	Security guards Sandwich
601.532	Expenses	Security guards Hamburguer
601.540	Expenses	Cleaning supplies
601.541	Expenses	Cleaning supplies Sandwich
601.542	Expenses	Cleaning supplies Hamburguer
601.550	Expenses	Stationery
601.551	Expenses	Stationery Sandwich
601.552	Expenses	Stationery Hamburguer
601.560	Expenses	Maintenance
601.561	Expenses	Maintenance Sandwich
601.562	Expenses	Maintenance Hamburguer
601.570	Expenses	Insurance
601.571	Expenses	Insurance Sandwich
601.572	Expenses	Insurance Hamburguer
601.580	Expenses	Other taxes
601.581	Expenses	Other taxes Sandwich
601.582	Expenses	Other taxes Hamburguer
601.610	Expenses	Marketing
601.611	Expenses	Marketing Sandwich
601.612	Expenses	Marketing Hamburguer
601.620	Expenses	Training
601.621	Expenses	Training Sandwich
601.622	Expenses	Training Hamburguer
601.720	Expenses	Freight
601.721	Expenses	Freight Sandwich
601.722	Expenses	Freight Hamburguer
613.010	Expenses	Depreciation
613.011	Expenses	Depreciation Sandwich
613.012	Expenses	Depreciation Hamburguer
700.000	Financial Expenses	Financial Expenses
701.040	Financial Expenses	Interests
701.100	Financial Expenses	Bank fees

* Figure 7

48

As you can see the number of accounts increased and this is what will help us to have more detail in the reports in a way that allows us to make better analyzes.

If you don't have a list of accounts in your business, you can use this list and add or remove the accounts required by your business.

Now we are going to record the information in the "system" that as we mentioned we can use Excel to do it. So let's make the format that we will use to make the records in Excel.

If you have Excel in your computer it would be good if you do this exercise as we are talking about it, since we can understand it in a better way if we write and follow the example in the "system". It is not necessary that you are an expert in Excel to be able to do the example, you only need to know the basics, since we will do it step by step in a simple way.

We must put it in a Database format, this means, to put columns without leaving spaces and fill down the information, also without leaving spaces.

First we will put the columns and for this we will include the Number of the record, Description, Quantity, Measure Unit, Business, then all the Assets, the sing of "=", all the Liabilities, the sign of "+", All Equity accounts, Validation, Cash Flow, Concept, Income / Cost / Expense, Account.

#	Description	Quantity	MU	Business	Assets	=	Liabilities	+	Equity		Cash Flow	Concept	Inc/Cost/Exp	Account

*Figure 8

In the Assets, Liabilities and Equity columns, each account must be included. This format may not make sense to you at the beginning, but it has a reason why to order it in this way that we will understand later. Now we'll start with the filling of the information.

We will make the example with 30 records, which could be a lot, but they are necessary to be able to see the reports in a better way and with those 30 registers you will have a clear understanding on how to make the records, so that you can do it in your business immediately. Some of the records are going to be grouped to make it faster. In this example we are not going to include taxes so we can make it simple.

The rules that we must follow to fill the file are the following:

* The fields of "Quantity" and "Measure Unit" are for products only, if it's not related to a product, we put NA (not applicable).

* All records have at least two movements (transactions as the CPA's say), either in the Assets, Liabilities or Capital side. This is where we'll require practice to do it better each time.

* The "Validation" column must be zero and it is the subtraction of Assets minus Liabilities and Equity. We can put a formula in this cell to make the calculation automatically and reduce the possibility of an error.

* The columns "Cash Flow" and "Concept" are only filled when there is an amount in the Banks (Assets) column, in not we put NA.

* The columns of "Income / Cost / Expense" and "Account" are only filled when there is an amount in the column "Retained Earnings" (Equity), if not we put NA.

If you don't understand this rules, don't worry, we are going to talk about it when we make the records.

RECORDS

In this part we must have a lot of patience, since it is probable that at the beginning we don't understand it and we'll need to read it again and go several times to **Figure 10** where we have all the records of the complete example. But if we continue doing the exercise, at the end we will know how to make the registers and perform analyzes.

If for any reason after reading several times the records you don't understand how to do it, you can skip this part and copy the information where we have all the records (Figure 10) in an Excel sheet, so you can make the analyzes.

This part of recording is usually made by the accountant or the administrative assistant, but it is good that we know how they are done.

To make it more understandable, when we talk about the columns in which we will record information, we will put them in *UPPERCASE*.

Record 1. We open the business with the owner giving $ 10,000 in Cash. We put "1" in the *RECORD NUMBER*, in the *DESCRIPTION* we put "Open company". As it isn't a product we put "NA" in *QUANTITY* and *MEASURE UNIT*. Nor it's related to any of the Businesses that are Sandwich (S) or Hamburger (H) so we put "NA" in *BUSINESS*. In the column of *BANKS* we put 10,000 because we got that amount to start the business in cash and as we said before, there should be two records, the second one is in *OWNER'S INVESTMENT* since is what the owner gave to the business.

The **VALIDATION** column is a formula that includes Assets less Liabilities and less Equity, in this example in Assets there are 10,000 (Banks), in Liabilities there is nothing and in Equity there are 10,000 (Owner's investment). Therefore it is zero because 10,000 - 0 – 10,000 = 0.

Because the Banks column has an amount (10,000), we must put information in the **CASH FLOW** and **CONCEPT** column, which in this example would be "Financing" (as it is a Financing operation) and "Starting".

As there is no amount in the **RETAINED EARNINGS** column (which at this point we have not even used that account), we put "NA" in **INCOME/COST/EXPENSE** and in the **ACCOUNT**.

So the record would look like the following image:

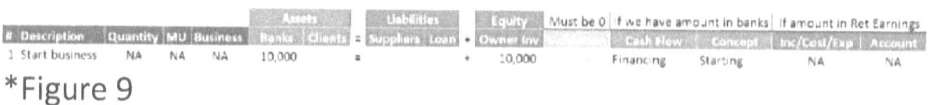

*Figure 9

The other records are made in the same way and I will not make the explanation with all the detail that we did in the previous one to not make it too long. At the end of all the record I will include a Figure so you can see how it should look (**Figure 10**) and compare it with the records you are doing in excel.

The Assets, Liabilities and Equity accounts that we are going to include in Excel will only be the ones we will use in this example so we don't to make a long file so we can and be able to look at it better.

* You can Copy the columns as they are on **Figure 10** to make filling easier.

Record 2. The equipment to make the Sandwiches and Hamburgers is purchased for $ 6,000. It is not related to Products or **BUSINESS UNIT**. In **BANKS** (Assets) we put -6,000 because it is an outflow of money and in **FIXED ASSETS** 6,000 (Assets). There is an amount in Banks, so we put "Investment" in **CASH FLOW** and in **CONCEPT** we put "Machinery". There is no amount in **RETAINED EARNINGS**, so the last two columns are "NA".

If you have doubts about how to do this, you can go forward where the records of the 30 transactions are (**Figure 10**), you can do the same with the following records.

From now on what is related to Sandwich we will put only the letter "S" and what is related to Hamburger only the letter "H".

Records 3, 4, 5 and 6. Purchase of materials to make 2,000 S and 2,000 H. Bread S for a total of $ 500 (price of each bread $ 0.25), Ham for $ 750 (price sliced ham $ 0.40), Bread H for $ 800 (unit price $ 0.38) and Meat for $ 1,250 (unit price $ 0.63).

We will record these amounts separately in **BANKS** and with a negative sign because they are cash outflows and on the other hand we register the same amounts in the **INVENTORIES** column of **EACH PRODUCT**. In the column of **CASH FLOW** it is "Operational" and **CONCEPT** is "Materials".

Record 7. Sale paid in cash of 1,200 S at $ 1.60 each, income of $ 1,920. It is recorded in **BANKS** and in **RETAINED EARNINGS**. All Sales, Costs and Expenses will be included in Retained Earnings. In **CASH FLOW** it is "Operation". In **CONCEPT** it is "Sale". *In* **INCOME/COST/EXPENSE** it is "Income" and in **ACCOUNT** it is also "Income".

Records 8 and 9. This is related with the previous record, since in order to make the sale we take 1,200 units of Bread and Ham.

For Bread S the amount is $ 300 (1,200 for $ 0.25 it costs). It is with a negative sign in the **INVENTORY** and with a negative sign in **RETAINED EARNINGS**. As there is no amount in **BANKS** the **CASH FLOW** column and **CONCEPT** go with "NA". In **INCOME/COST/EXPENSE** it is "Cost" and in **ACCOUNT** it is "Material Cost". The same calculation for Ham, but with the cost of $ 0.40 per slice.

Record 10. Sale of cash of 1,000 H at $ 1.90 each with total income of $ 1,900. The way to make it is the same as register 7.

Records 11 and 12. It is to reduce the material of the Inventory and is the same procedure as for registers 8 and 9.

Record 13. Sale on Credit of 600 S, Income of $ 960. It is registered in **CUSTOMERS** and in **RETAINED EARNINGS**.

Records 14 and 15. Are for the inventory output. They way to make them is like 8 and 9 only that the amounts are for 600 units.

Record 16. Sale on Credit of 700 H, Income of $ 1,330. It is recorded in **CUSTOMERS** and in **RETAINED EARNINGS**.

Records 17 and 18. Are for the inventory output. They way to make them is like 11 and 12 only that the amounts are for 700 units.

Records 19 and 20. We have a person who makes the S and H, we consider him as a Direct Labor (Cost), he works part time and we pay him in this example $ 1,000 dollars per month. We want to make the records in each product as mentioned in the theoretical part and for this purpose we measure time of the employee to make each product, we are going to say that it takes 40% of the time of the month in S and 60% in H, since the most time consuming activity is preparing meat for H.

Based on this, we make the recording and to make it easier we'll not consider taxes, social security and benefits. The registration is $ 400 as a decrease in Labor S in **CASH** and decrease in **RETAINED EARNINGS**. It is "Operation" in **CASH FLOW**, "Payroll" in **CONCEPT**. It is "Cost" and "Direct Labor." The same goes for the S record, but with $ 600.

Records 21 and 22. We have an office lease of $ 700 per month and we make the same allocation per business unit (40% S and 60% H). Therefore, for S we decrease in **CASH** and **RETAINED EARNINGS** of $ 280. It is "Operation" **CASH FLOW**. **CONCEPT** "Lease". It is a "Leasing Expense". The same goes for H, but with $ 420.

The best way to understand the allocation of expenses that are for both products such as lease, electricity, gas, etc. is to imagine as if we hire a third party or outsourcing that has the same equipment and personnel than us. As if we paid a lease for the equipment or labor, based on the time that we use them for each product separately.

Records 23 and 24. We register the electricity of the month for $ 300 dollars, however the invoice is paid in the following month. We make the same allocation per business unit (40% S and 60% H), so for S we put the $ 120 as **SUPPLIERS** and in **RETAINED EARNINGS**. It is a "Expense" of "Electricity." The same goes for H, but with $ 180.

Records 25 and 26. We pay Water for $ 50, we make the same allocation per business unit (40% S and 60% H). Therefore, for S we decrease in **CASH** and **RETAINED EARNINGS** $ 20. It is "Operation" in **CASH FLOW**. **CONCEPT** "Water". It is a "Water" **EXPENSE**. Same goes for H, but with $ 30.

Records 27 and 28. We record the owner's salary, we calculate it based on the salary of a part-time (few hours a day) supervisor for this kind of business and as in reality he doesn't get paid, we register $ 600 dollars and make the same allocation per unit of business (40% S and 60% H), so for S we put $ 240 as a **LOAN** and in **RETAINED EARNINGS**. It is an **EXPENSE** of "Salaries". The same goes for H, but with $ 360.

Records 29 and 30. We calculate the depreciation of the month based on the value of the equipment and divide it by the number of months that we estimate that we can use the equipment. In this example is $ 90 and is the amount that we will consider as depreciation. We make an allocation per business unit based in the time that the equipment is used by each product (56% S and 44% H), so for S we put $ 50 as

ACCUMULATED DEPRECIATION and *RETAINED EARNINGS*. It is a "Depreciation" *EXPENSE*. Same goes for H, but with $ 40.

Once that you made all the records, your Excel file should look like the following figure:

#	Description	Quantity	MU	Business	Assets: Bank	Assets: [illegible]	Assets: [illegible]	Assets: [illegible]	Assets: [illegible]	Assets: [illegible]	Assets: [illegible]	Assets: [illegible]	Liabilities: Suppliers	Liabilities: [illegible]	Equity: [illegible]	Equity: [illegible]	Cash Flow	Category	Inc/Cost/Exp	Account
1	Start business	N/A	NA	N/A	[illegible]										[illegible]		Financing	Starting	NA	NA
2	Buy equipment	N/A	NA	N/A	[illegible]							[illegible]					Investment	Machinery	NA	NA
3	Buy Bread S	2,000	pc	S	100		500										Operation	Materials	NA	NA
4	Buy Bread H	2,000	pc	H	750				750								Operation	Materials	NA	NA
5	Buy Ham	2,000	pc	[illegible]	800			[illegible]									Operation	Materials	NA	NA
6	Buy Meat	2,000	pc	H	1,240					1,240							Operation	Materials	NA	NA
7	Sale in cash S	1,200	pc	S	1,520											1,920	Operation	Sale	Income	Income
8	Sale in cash S	1,200	pc	S			300									300	NA	NA	Cost	Material Cost
9	Sale in cash	1,200	pc	[illegible]				[illegible]								480	NA	NA	Cost	Material Cost
10	Sale in cash H	1,000	pc	H	1,900											1,900	Operation	Sale	Income	Income
11	Sale in cash H	1,000	pc	H					375							375	NA	NA	Cost	Material Cost
12	Sale in cash H	1,000	pc	H						625						625	NA	NA	Cost	Material Cost
13	Sale in credit	600	pc	[illegible]		960										960	NA	NA	Income	Income
14	Sale in credit S	600	pc	S			150									150	NA	NA	Cost	Material Cost
15	Sale in credit S	600	pc	S				240								240	NA	NA	Cost	Material Cost
16	Sale in credit H	700	pc	H		[illegible]										[illegible]	NA	NA	Income	Income
17	Sale in credit H	700	pc	H					263							263	NA	NA	Cost	Material Cost
18	Sale in credit H	700	pc	H						438						438	NA	NA	Cost	Material Cost
19	Direct Labor S	N/A	NA	S	400											400	Operation	Payroll	Cost	Direct Labor
20	Direct Labor H	N/A	NA	H	[illegible]											[illegible]	Operation	Payroll	Cost	Direct Labor
21	Office Lease S	N/A	NA	S	280											280	Operation	Lease	Expense	Lease
22	Office Lease H	N/A	NA	H	420											420	Operation	Lease	Expense	Lease
23	Electricity S	N/A	NA	S									120			120	NA	NA	Expense	Electricity
24	Electricity H	N/A	NA	H									180			180	NA	NA	Expense	Electricity
25	Water S	N/A	NA	S	20											20	Operation	Water	Expense	Water
26	Water H	N/A	NA	H	30											30	Operation	Water	Expense	Water
27	Salaries S	N/A	NA	[illegible]										[illegible]		[illegible]	NA	NA	Expense	Salaries
28	Salaries H	N/A	NA	H										360		360	NA	NA	Expense	Salaries
29	Depreciation S	N/A	NA	S								50				50	NA	NA	Expense	Depreciation
30	Depreciation H	N/A	NA	H								40				40	NA	NA	Expense	Depreciation

*Figure 10

This Figure 10 is included in a bigger size at the end of the book (Appendix 1).

Compare your Excel file with the previous image. If something is different, correct it.

In real life, more columns must be included in this file to have the complete information, such as a column for the date of the record, that we can use to make analyzes and comparisons per month. Another column we need to include is the account number that we define in the list of accounts. But in this example we'll leave it this way so we don't make the file more extensive.

Now let's make the Reports or Financial Statements with this information.

REPORTS WITH PIVOT TABLES

𝔚e will select the information on the sheet where we made all the records, which is from cell A2 through X32, it is important that when we make pivot tables all fields have a title, at least one letter. Otherwise Excel will not allow us to make the pivot table.

We click on the Menu "Insert" - PivotTable, the following alert will appear automatically in which the cells we chose will be in the "Table/Range" section. We click on "OK" so the pivot table can be displayed on another sheet.

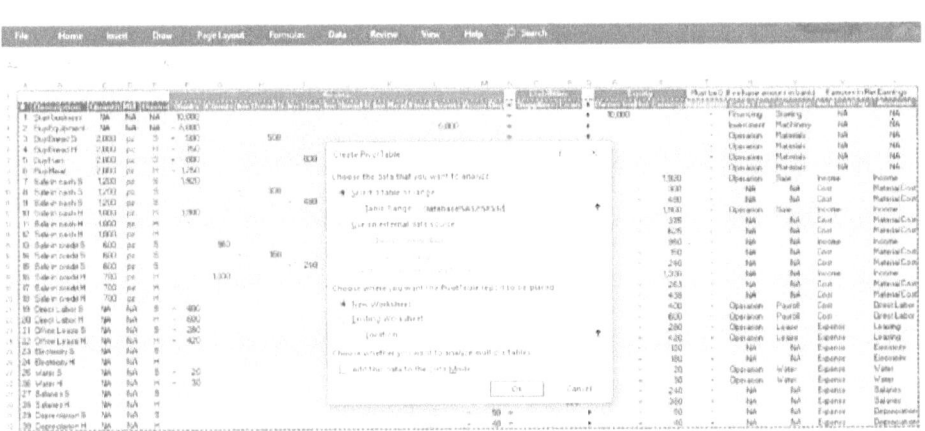

*Figure 11

A new sheet will be opened with an image like the following:

*Figure 12

The box on the right is the part where the pivot table is designed, in the four fields below it is where we will indicate what information we want and how we need to see it. There we can put report filters, the information we want sorted by columns, what we want by rows and values.

We must make a good design of the pivot table, since the objective is that we do not need to do it again, that is, that we only make the pivot tables once and then the information is updated automatically when we make more records on the database sheet in following months.

We are going to make several kinds of pivot tables with the different Reports (Financial Statements). The first one that we are going to do is the Balance Sheet and we will include all the accounts of the assets, liabilities and equity in the box of values.

To do this we select each field (one by one) and drag it to the Values field, the table will take the form of the following image:

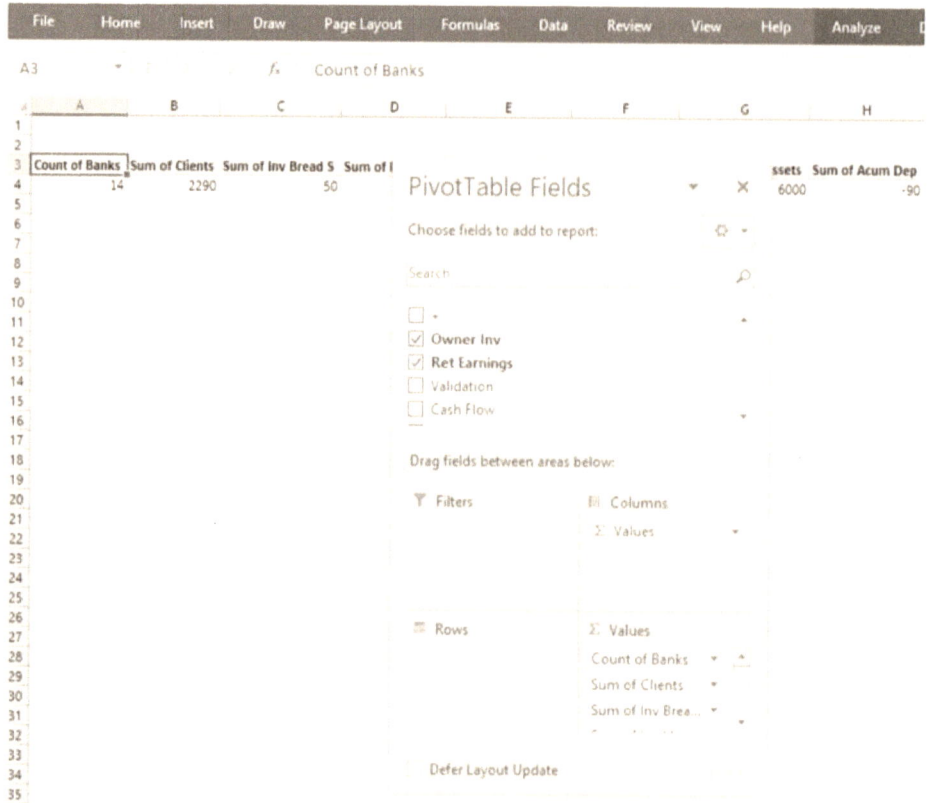

A3 | f_x | Count of Banks

	A	B	C	D	E	F	G	H
3	Count of Banks	Sum of Clients	Sum of Inv Bread S	Sum of I				ssets Sum of Acum Dep
4	14	2290		50			6000	-90

PivotTable Fields ▾ ✕

Choose fields to add to report: ✿ ▾

Search 🔎

☐ ·
☑ Owner Inv
☑ Ret Earnings
☐ Validation
☐ Cash Flow

Drag fields between areas below:

▼ Filters   ▦ Columns
                   Σ Values ▾

▦ Rows   Σ Values
                   Count of Banks ▾
                   Sum of Clients ▾
                   Sum of Inv Brea... ▾

Defer Layout Update

*Figure 13

It is likely that, as shown in the first columns (banks), the fields are set to "Count" instead of "Sum". We can see this because at the beginning of the title it says "Count of Banks" and it is necessary to change it since it tells us that we have 14, that is that we have fourteen records, but we do not want to see the quantity of registers, but the sum of all of them. So we must change it and to do this we select the field (Count of Banks), right click, select "value field settings" - Sum and the field will look like the following image.

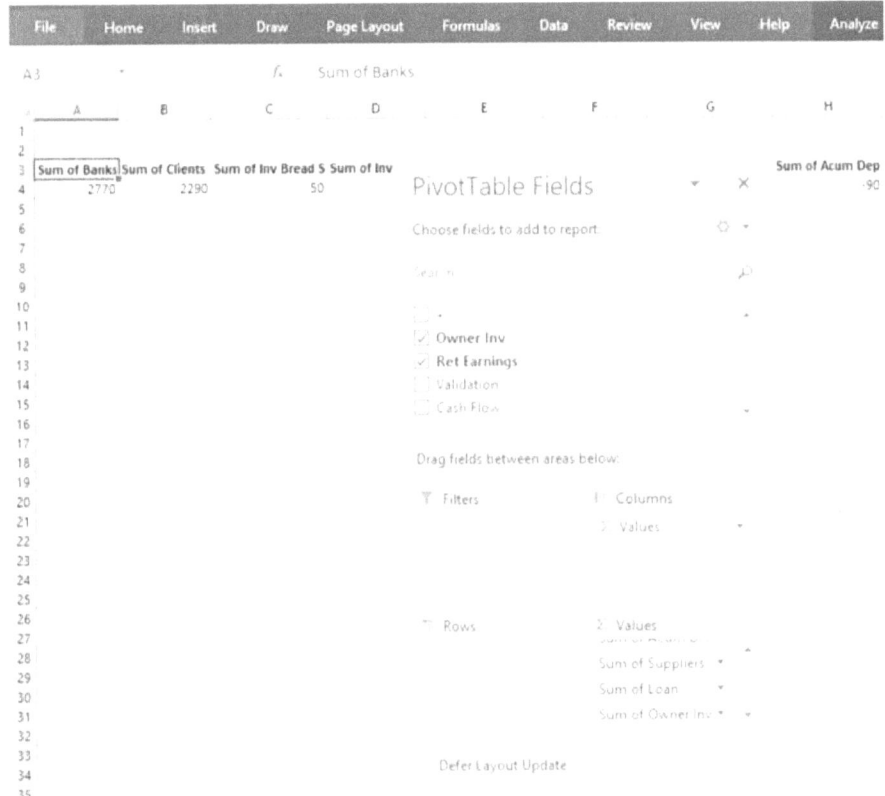

*Figure 14

Here we can select the "number format" which is the button in the lower left of the box where we can put it with commas and decimals.

The same must be done for all assets, liabilities and equity accounts. The sheet would look like the following image.

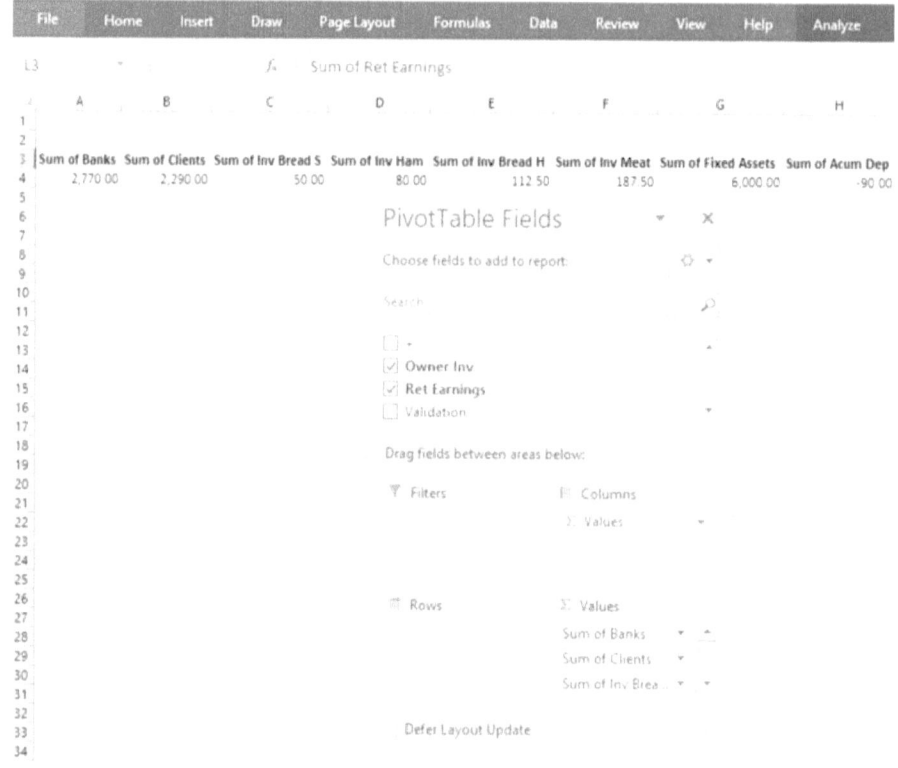

*Figure 15

If you struggle to make this pivot table or any of the others we will see, I can gladly send you the file in Excel if you request it by email at cpcarlosramos@cprqconsultoria.com, so that you compare the information with the one of your file and correct it.

Note: Pivot tables can be made in several ways, practically how each person wants to see the information. The information that someone wants to see in columns, another person prefers to see it in rows or in filters. The important thing is that we can include the information we need to perform analyzes.

Below the dynamic table we put the format in which we want to see the report. This is done only once, since we will link it to the pivot table and by updating the pivot table, the report will also be updated.

We put the Assets on the left and Liabilities and Equity on the right. We can give format the titles with blue background and white letters to visualize it better. Then we link each field to the pivot table, for example, in the banks cell we put the sign "=", we select the cell of the pivot table where the Banks value is and we click "enter".

The field should look like the following image:

A20 f_x Banks

	A	B	C	D	E
1					
2					
3	Sum of Banks	Sum of Clieı	Sum of Inv Bread S	Sum of Inv Hä	Sum of Inv Bread H
4	2,770.00	2,290.00	50.00	80.00	112.50
5					
6					
7	ASSETS		LIABILITIES		
8	Banks	2,770.00	Suppliers	300.00	
9	Clients	2,290.00	Loan	600.00	
10	Inventory Bread S	50.00	TOTAL LIABILITIES	900.00	
11	Inventory Ham	80.00			
12	Inventory Bread H	112.50	EQUITY		
13	Inventory Meat	187.50	Owner Investment	10,000.00	
14	Fixed Assets	6,000.00	Retained Earnings	500.00	
15	Acum Depreciation -	90.00	TOTAL EQUITY	10,500.00	
16					
17	TOTAL ASSETS	11,400.00	LIABILITIES + EQUITY	11,400.00	
18					

*Figure 16

We do the same with the other accounts, only in the cells of Total Assets, Total Liabilities, Total Equity and Liabilities + Equity we put a sum with the sum function Σ that is in the start menu.

Here we can begin to see the numbers of the business and make metrics that we can analyze each month, as an example we can see that the Clients (what the Clients owe us) are greater than the Suppliers (what we owe to the Suppliers), what it is not good because it means that Clients are getting more leverage with our money, than we do with our suppliers and we can put a metric for it that we can name it Customer metric.

Customer Metric = Customers / Suppliers

Customer Metric = 2,290 / 300 = 7.6

The goal is that we this number to one or less than one, this means that what customers owe us should be less than what we owe to suppliers, so in this case we are far from it and we must look for actions that let us achieve our goal.

There are accounts such as Banks and Retained Earnings in which it is necessary to see more detail to have a clearer picture of the business and that is why the other reports are made.

Let's make the Report to see the detail of Banks called Cash Flow.

We do the same as for the previous pivot table, we select the "Insert" Menu - Pivot Table, the following alert will appear automatically in which the cells we chose will be in the "Table/Range" section. We click on "OK" so the pivot table can be displayed on another sheet.

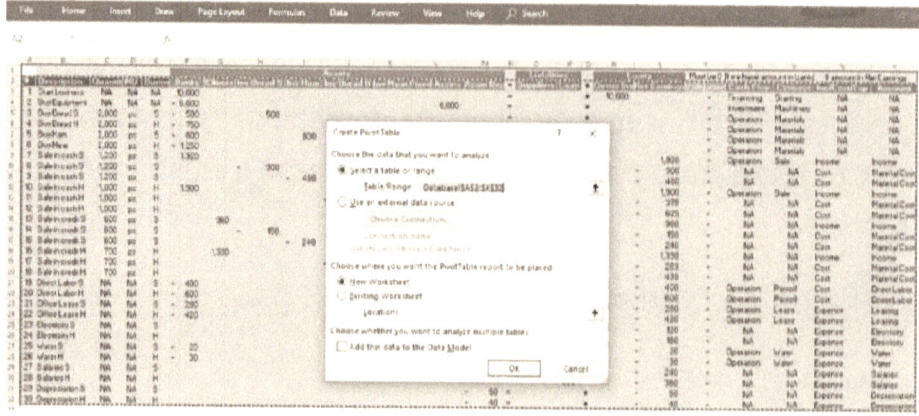

*Figure 17

A new sheet will be opened with an image like the following:

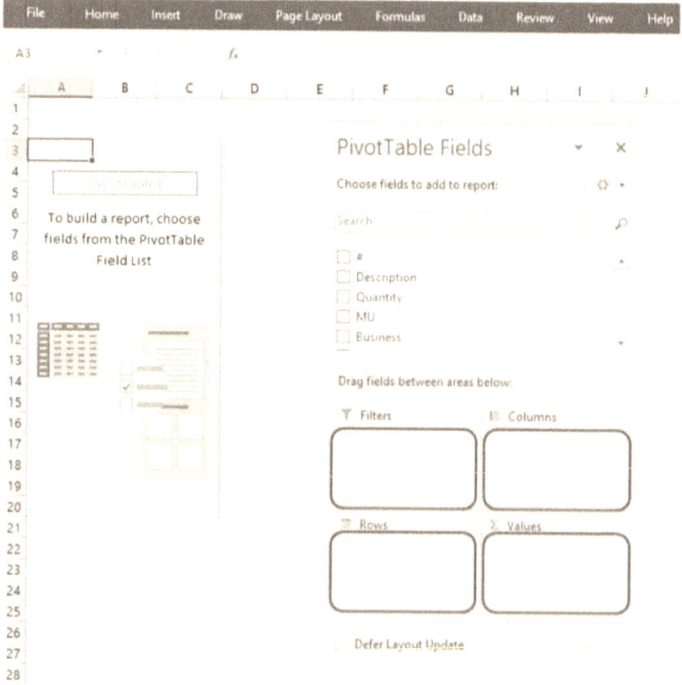

*Figure 18

In this report we will drag the Cash Flow and Concept fields in the "Rows" box. And in the "Values" box, the Banks field.

The information in the Banks field could set by default as "Count", we do the same as the previous table to put it as "Sum". To do this we right click, we select "value field settings" - Sum.

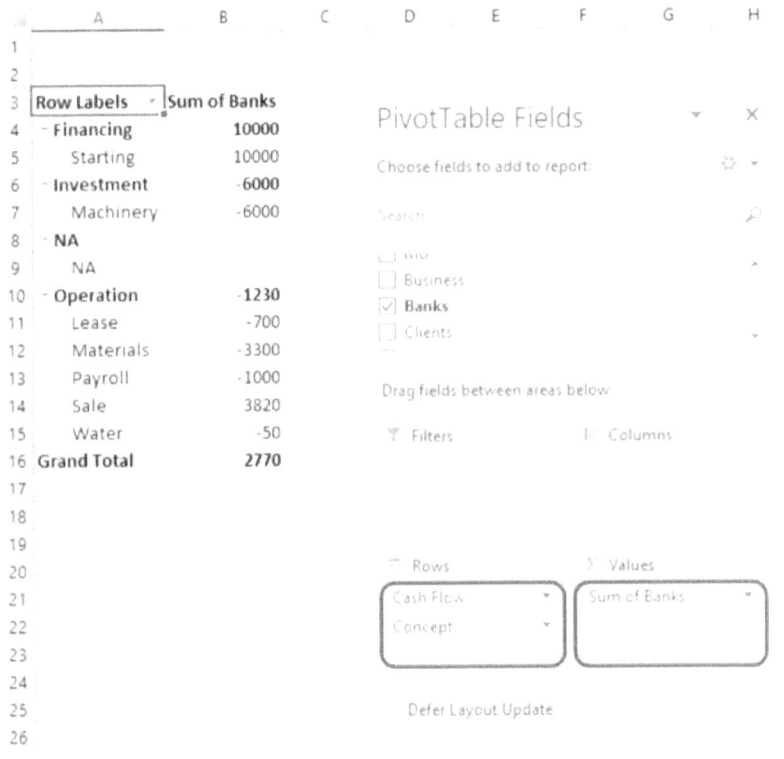

*Figure 19

We can give a better format to the table, to do it we go to the Design Menu - Report Layout – Show in Tabular Form.

*Figure 20

We can sort the table to put the Operation first, then Investment and at the end Financing Cash Flow. We can do this by dragging the Operation cell up and moving the others in the same way.

Also in the Concept column we sort it in a way that the sale is the first concept, then materials and then the other concepts.

The report would be as follows:

Cash Flow	Concept	Sum of Banks
Operation	Lease	-700.00
	Materials	-3,300.00
	Payroll	-1,000.00
	Sale	3,820.00
	Water	-50.00
Operation Total		**-1,230.00**
Investment	Machinery	-6,000.00
Investment Total		**-6,000.00**
Financing	Starting	10,000.00
Financing Total		**10,000.00**
NA	NA	
NA Total		
Grand Total		**2,770.00**

*Figure 21

With this information we can make more analysis, since we can see that although we have $ 41,600 pesos in the Bank, the cash flow from the Operation is negative in $ 1,230 dollars and that is not good, so we must make decisions to correct it and avoid the risk of running out of money.

Now let's look at the Income Statement.

We do the same as in the previous pivot tables, we select the Insert Menu - Pivot Table, the following alert will appear automatically in which the cells we chose will be in the "Table/Range" section. We click on "OK" so the pivot table can be displayed on another sheet.

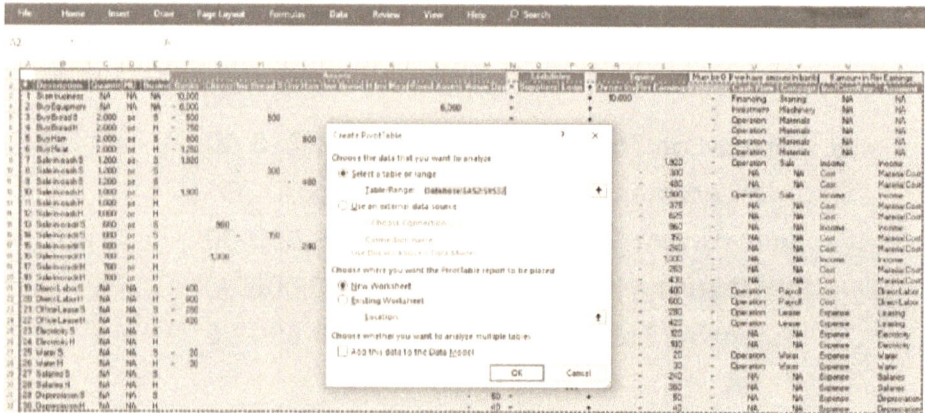

*Figure 22

A new sheet will be opened with an image like the following:

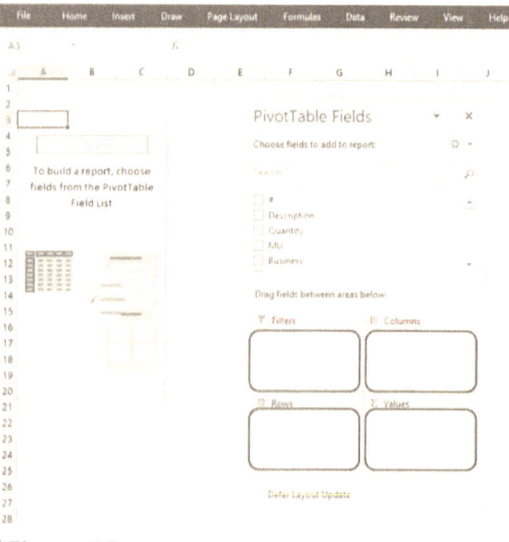

*Figure 23

In this report we will drag in the "Rows" box the fields of "Income / Cost / Expense" and "Account". In the "Values" box, the "Retained Earnings" field.

*Figure 24

The information in the field of Retained Earnings could be set by default as "Count", if this happens we do the same as the previous pivot table to put it as "Sum". To do it we right click, select "value field settings" - Sum

We can give a better format to the table, to do it we go to the Design Menu - Report Layout – Show in Tabular Form.

We can also sort it to include Income first, then Costs and then Expenses. We do this by dragging the Income, Cost and Expenses cells up or down, as we want. The same can be done to sort the account column where we can put at the beginning the Salaries, then Leasing and then the other accounts.

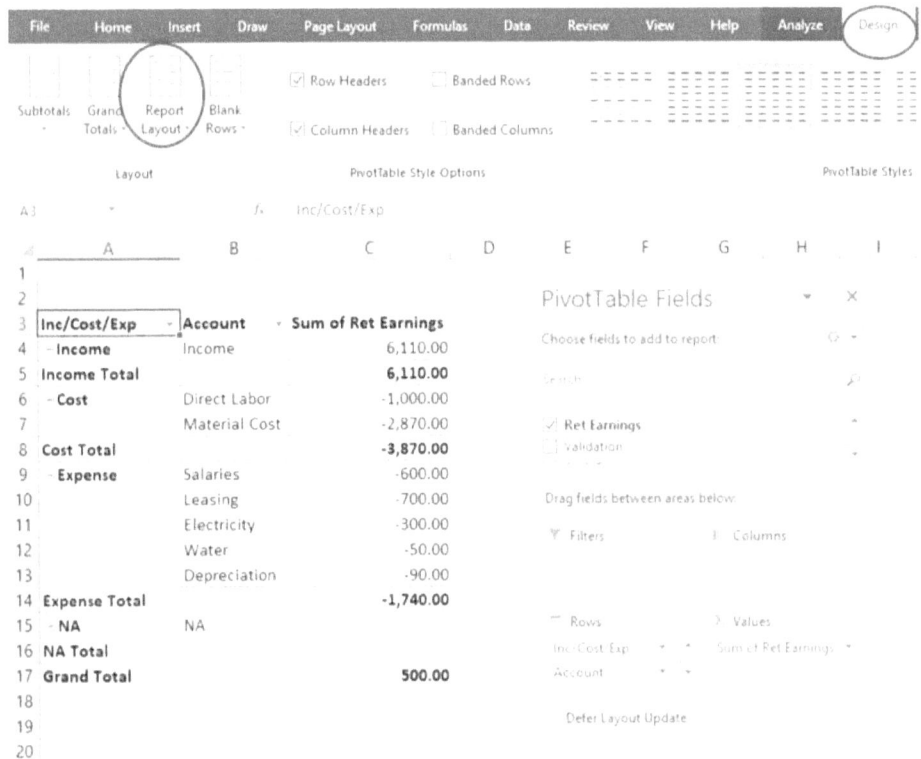

	A	B	C	D	E	F	G	H	I
1									
2						PivotTable Fields		▾	✕
3	Inc/Cost/Exp	Account	Sum of Ret Earnings			Choose fields to add to report:			⚙ ▾
4	- Income	Income	6,110.00						
5	Income Total		6,110.00						
6	- Cost	Direct Labor	-1,000.00						
7		Material Cost	-2,870.00			✓ Ret Earnings			
8	Cost Total		-3,870.00			Validation			
9	- Expense	Salaries	-600.00						
10		Leasing	-700.00			Drag fields between areas below:			
11		Electricity	-300.00			▼ Filters		‖ Columns	
12		Water	-50.00						
13		Depreciation	-90.00						
14	Expense Total		-1,740.00						
15	- NA	NA				≡ Rows		Σ Values	
16	NA Total					Inc/Cost/Exp ▾ ▾		Sum of Ret Earnings ▾	
17	Grand Total		500.00			Account ▾ ▾			
18									
19						Defer Layout Update			
20									

*Figure 25

At the bottom of this table is a field that says NA, since this part has no quantity, we can remove it and to do it we can click in the button on the right side of the cell "Inc / Cost / Exp" and deselect the field NA.

The report would be as follows:

	Inc/Cost/Exp	Account	Sum of Ret Earnings
3	Inc/Cost/Exp	⊤ Account	⌄ Sum of Ret Earnings
4	– Income	Income	6,110.00
5	Income Total		6,110.00
6	– Cost	Direct Labor	-1,000.00
7		Material Cost	-2,870.00
8	Cost Total		-3,870.00
9	– Expense	Salaries	-600.00
10		Leasing	-700.00
11		Electricity	-300.00
12		Water	-50.00
13		Depreciation	-90.00
14	Expense Total		-1,740.00
15	Grand Total		500.00

*Figure 26

With this information we can see that we have a profit of $ 500 dollars and we can calculate some metrics as the percentage of profit between the sales that in this example is 8% (500 / 6,110) that we can compare against other businesses of our same industry.

We can also see the percentage of Profit between the investment (the investment is taken from the Balance Sheet report) and that is 5% monthly (500 / 10,000). That is the interest that the money we invest is giving us, so we can compare it against what the Bank or some other investment would give us with this same amount of money.

But with this reports we cannot see more detailed analyzes that allow us to know in which products we earn more, the breakeven point, etc. And this is what normally happens when we record the information for tax purposes.

But we did recorded in detail, so it is only a matter of including another field to the report so we can have more detailed information and be able to make the analyzes we want.

To do this we will only need to include in the same pivot table one more field in the "Columns" box and that is the Business field.

*Figure 27

The report would be as follows:

3 Sum of Ret Earnin			Business		
4 Inc/Cost/Exp	.т Account	▾ H		S	Grand Total
5 −Income	Income		3,230.00	2,880.00	6,110.00
6 Income Total			3,230.00	2,880.00	6,110.00
7 −Cost	Direct Labor		-600.00	-400.00	-1,000.00
8	Material Cost		-1,700.00	-1,170.00	-2,870.00
9 Cost Total			-2,300.00	-1,570.00	-3,870.00
10 −Expense	Salaries		-360.00	-240.00	-600.00
11	Leasing		-420.00	-280.00	-700.00
12	Electricity		-180.00	-120.00	-300.00
13	Water		-30.00	-20.00	-50.00
14	Depreciation		-40.00	-50.00	-90.00
15 Expense Total			-1,030.00	-710.00	-1,740.00
16 Grand Total			-100.00	600.00	500.00

*Figure 28

Now we can see in this report in which product we earn more, which in this example are the Sandwiches (S) that although the sale is lower than the Burgers (H), the profit of S is $ 600 and in H we have a loss of $ 100. There is a very big difference between the earnings of one product and the other (in this example a loss in one of the products) and based on this you can make decisions such as advertising towards a certain product and do more analysis on some expenses derived from the time that it is dedicated to each product, how to reduce expenses, simplify processes, reduce times, etc.

This kind of situations in which there are products with loss is very common in business, since some products subsidize others and as in the Total we have profits, we do not pay attention to details by product. However, if we analyze it in this way and manage to eliminate the loss in that product, we will automatically increase the profits.

SUMMARY

If we put the three Reports to analyze them we have the following picture:

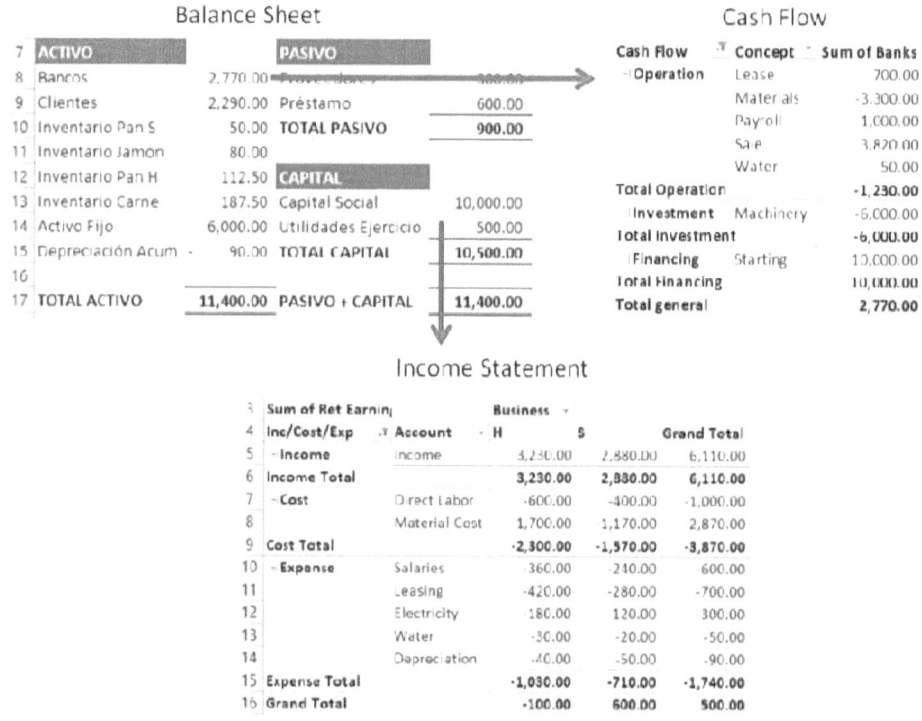

Balance Sheet

7	**ACTIVO**	**PASIVO**	
8	Bancos	2.770.00 Proveedores	300.00
9	Clientes	2.290.00 Préstamo	600.00
10	Inventario Pan S	50.00 **TOTAL PASIVO**	**900.00**
11	Inventario Jamón	80.00	
12	Inventario Pan H	112.50 **CAPITAL**	
13	Inventario Carne	187.50 Capital Social	10,000.00
14	Activo Fijo	6,000.00 Utilidades Ejercicio	500.00
15	Depreciación Acum -	90.00 **TOTAL CAPITAL**	**10,500.00**
16			
17	**TOTAL ACTIVO**	**11,400.00 PASIVO + CAPITAL**	**11,400.00**

Cash Flow

Cash Flow	Concept	Sum of Banks
Operation	Lease	700.00
	Materials	-3.300.00
	Payroll	1,000.00
	Sale	3.820.00
	Water	50.00
Total Operation		-1,230.00
Investment	Machinery	-6,000.00
Total Investment		-6,000.00
Financing	Starting	10,000.00
Total Financing		10,000.00
Total general		2,770.00

Income Statement

	Sum of Ret Earning		Business		
3					
4	Inc/Cost/Exp	Account	H	S	Grand Total
5	- Income	Income	3,230.00	2,880.00	6,110.00
6	Income Total		3,230.00	2,880.00	6,110.00
7	- Cost	Direct Labor	-600.00	-400.00	-1,000.00
8		Material Cost	1,700.00	1,170.00	2,870.00
9	Cost Total		-2,300.00	-1,570.00	-3,870.00
10	- Expense	Salaries	360.00	210.00	600.00
11		Leasing	-420.00	-280.00	-700.00
12		Electricity	180.00	120.00	300.00
13		Water	-30.00	-20.00	-50.00
14		Depreciation	40.00	-50.00	-90.00
15	Expense Total		-1,030.00	-710.00	-1,740.00
16	Grand Total		-100.00	600.00	500.00

*Figure 29

Personally, I like to see the Income Statement first to know if we are winning or losing and in which products we earn more than in others or even in which products we lose (which is a common situation in many businesses), to take the necessary actions such as advertise more of certain product, reduce costs or times in another or even stop producing a product if that is the best option.

When we see the Cash Flow we realize that the operation had a negative flow and when we see the Balance Sheet we see that what the Customers owe us is very high compared to what we owe to suppliers, so we should look to collect faster to customers or request credits from suppliers so we can have a positive cash flow.

These and the analyzes mentioned above, will help us to see the picture of our business and if we do it constantly every month, reviewing the metrics that we mentioned, we can make decisions that help us increase profits.

I hope that with this example you have a clear way to make the records and analyzes in your business and that you can apply it immediately to make the right decisions and increase your profits.

* Note: If you require the excel file we were working with (which includes the listings, pivot tables, etc.), I can gladly send it to you if you request it to my email cpcarlosramos@cprqconsultoria.com

* Repeat the example since the recording, the second time will be easier, only practice will make it easier.

APPENDIX 1

#	Description	Quantity	MU	Business	Banks	Clients	Inv Bread S	Inv Ham	Inv Bread H	Inv Meat	Fixed Assets	Accum Dep
1	Start business	NA	NA	NA	10,000							
2	Buy Equipment	NA	NA	NA	6,000						6,000	
3	Buy Bread S	2,000	pz	S	500		500					
4	Buy Bread H	2,000	pz	H	750				750			
5	Buy Ham	2,000	pz	S	800			800				
6	Buy Meat	2,000	pz	H						1,250		
7	Sale in cash S	1,200	pz	S	1,250							
8	Sale in cash S	1,200	pz	S	1,920							
9	Sale in cash S	1,200	pz	S			300	480				
10	Sale in cash H	1,000	pz	H								
11	Sale in cash H	1,000	pz	H	1,900				375	625		
12	Sale in cash H	1,000	pz	H								
13	Sale in credit S	600	pz	S								
14	Sale in credit S	600	pz	S		960						
15	Sale in credit S	600	pz	S			150	240				
16	Sale in credit H	700	pz	H								
17	Sale in credit H	700	pz	H		1,330						
18	Sale in credit H	700	pz	H					263	438		
19	Direct Labor S	NA	NA	S	400							
20	Direct Labor H	NA	NA	H	600							
21	Office Lease S	NA	NA	S	280							
22	Office Lease H	NA	NA	H	420							
23	Electricity S	NA	NA	S								
24	Electricity H	NA	NA	H								
25	Water S	NA	NA	S	20							
26	Water H	NA	NA	H	30							
27	Salaries S	NA	NA	S								
28	Salaries H	NA	NA	H								
29	Depreciation S	NA	NA	S								50
30	Depreciation H	NA	NA	H								40

Supplier	Loan	Owner Inv	Ret Earnings	Must be 0	Cash Flow	Category	Inc/Cost/Exp	Account
		10,000			Financing	Starting	NA	NA
			1,920		Investment	Machinery	NA	NA
			300		Operation	Materials	Cost	Material Cost
			480		Operation	Materials	Cost	Material Cost
			1,900		Operation	Materials	Cost	Material Cost
			375		Operation	Sale	Income	Income
			625		NA	NA	Cost	Material Cost
			960		NA	NA	Income	Income
			150		NA	NA	Cost	Material Cost
			240		NA	NA	Income	Income
			1,330		NA	NA	Cost	Material Cost
			263		NA	NA	Income	Income
			438		NA	NA	Cost	Material Cost
			400		Operation	Payroll	Cost	Direct Labor
			600		Operation	Payroll	Cost	Direct Labor
			280		Operation	Lease	Expense	Leasing
			420		Operation	Lease	Expense	Leasing
120			120		Operation	NA	Expense	Electricity
180			180		Operation	NA	Expense	Electricity
			20		Operation	Water	Expense	Water
			30		Operation	Water	Expense	Water
	240		240		Operation	NA	Expense	Salaries
	360		360		Operation	NA	Expense	Salaries
			50		NA	NA	Expense	Depreciation
			40		NA	NA	Expense	Depreciation

BIBLIOGRAPHY

* Business Valuation with Excel. Probabilistic Simulation

    Werner Zitzmann Riedler.

    Alfaomega editorial.

* Learn formulas and functions with Excel.

    With 100 practical examples.

    Alfaomega editorial.

* Images of search engines as Freepik, Storyblocks y Unplash.

ABOUT THE AUTHOR

CARL RAMQUIÑONY

CPA with a Master's Degree in Finance, graduated from ITESM Campus Monterrey, with more than 20 years of experience in the Finance area (Finance Director, Controller, Accounting Manager, Business Consultant) in both Public and Private companies. In Industries such as Automobile, Manufacturing, Ceramics, Mining, Services, Restaurants, Medical, Financial Companies, Marketing Firms and others. With international experience, leading companies from Detroit Michigan and Salt Lake City, Utah.

Consultant in the Firm CPRQ Consulting.

Writer of book Orientation to Accounting for Non-Accountants.

YouTube channel CPRQ Consultoria and CPRQ Consulting with free videos in English and Spanish of Finance topics.

Webinar of How to identify losses to increase profits.

Participation in RCG Television programs of Business Finances and Personal Finances.

www.ingramcontent.com/pod-product-compliance
Lightning Source LLC
Chambersburg PA
CBHW020602220526
45463CB00006B/2414